T0010599

STRANGE BUT TRUE STORIES

BOOK 1

The Presidential Ghost

Mystery Spots on Earth

UFO or Weather Balloon?

...and More!

Janice Greene

SADDLEBACK
EDUCATIONAL PUBLISHING

STRANGE BUT TRUE STORIES

BOOK 1

The Presidential Ghost
Mystery Spots on Earth
UFO or Weather Balloon?

BOOK 2

Bob Lazar, the UFO Guy
The Mothman Mystery
Mischievous Spirits

BOOK 3

Phantom Ships
The Jersey Devil
Living Dinosaurs?

BOOK 4

Skulls of Doom
Winchester Mystery House
What Lurks Beneath the Waves?

BOOK 5

King Tut's Curse
Amazing Athletic Feats
Monster or Myth?

...and More!

SADDLEBACK
EDUCATIONAL PUBLISHING
www.sdlback.com

ISBN-13: 978-1-61651-765-6
ISBN-10: 1-61651-765-4
eBook: 978-1-61247-296-6

Printed in Guangzhou, China
NOR/0614/CA21400939

18 17 16 15 14   5 6 7 8 9

CONTENTS

Steer Clear of These Addresses!

What a Way to Go!

STRANGE BUT TRUE STORIES

THE ROSWELL MYSTERY

Sometime during the first week of July 1947, *something* crashed near the town of Roswell, New Mexico. To this day there's disagreement about whether it was a weather balloon or an alien spacecraft.

Several people in Roswell said they'd seen a burning object pass over the town. The next day, Mac Brazel was herding sheep when he saw the wreck for himself. It was about the size of a football field!

He picked up pieces of the wreckage and showed them to his neighbors, the Proctors. Loretta Proctor said one scrap "looked like lightweight wood." Brazel and Proctor tried to cut it and burn it, but they couldn't make a mark in it. "It was different from anything we'd ever seen," Brazel said. "Some of the material was like aluminum foil. But when it was crushed, it would straighten itself out!" Another piece of the wreck had purplish pink figures on it. It reminded him of writing. But it didn't look like any language he'd ever seen.

Mac Brazel went into Roswell to report the wreck to the sheriff. Then the sheriff called the Roswell Army Air Field. Loretta Proctor remembers that Brazel was held at the army base for a week. "After Mac Brazel came back," she said, "his story had changed. 'Well, they say it was a weather balloon,' he said. And that's all he would say about it."

Frank Kaufmann, an officer at the Roswell Army Air Field, remembers the crash, too. "The radar screen lit up," he recalls. "Then calls started coming in from people driving on highway 285. They said they'd seen 'some kind of flame going down.'"

Kaufmann immediately went to see base commander Col. William Blanchard. A search party was formed.

Kaufmann was in the search party. "It was pitch black," he said. "Off the highway, we could see this kind of glow. From 200 to 300 yards away, it didn't look like a plane or a missile or anything like that. We radioed for the specialists—the chemical boys—to inspect the area. When they told us it was all right to go in, we got our first close look at the debris.

"We were . . . just dumbfounded. We didn't know what to think. And we couldn't help wondering how people would react if we told them what we saw. They'd probably think we were out of our minds.

"They were good-looking people, with ash-colored faces and skin. About five feet four, five feet five. Small ears, small noses. Fine features. Hairless. There were five in all. I saw just two of them. One was thrown out of the craft itself. And one was half in and half out of the cabin. Did I mention they were all dead?

"I didn't go near the craft itself. I just

took a quick look because we were so busy. Our job was to truck everything out of there before daylight. The craft was small. I'd say it must have been 20 to 22 feet long and maybe 10 to 12 feet wide. The strange thing was that the craft carried no fuel. It seemed to be powered by a series of octagon-shaped cells.

"When one of the men noticed that the aliens' skin was deteriorating, we placed them in body bags. The bodies were the first to go, then the craft.

"It's something you live with all your life. You can't erase it from your mind. Seeing those bodies and seeing the craft— we're not alone."

Kaufmann and the other soldiers went back to the base. The men were warned never to talk about the crash. Kaufmann said nothing about it until the 1990s. Then other witnesses also began talking about that strange event in 1947.

One of those witnesses was Glenn Dennis, a man who worked at a funeral home in Roswell. He said that a man from the base called about the availability of five child-sized caskets. Dennis asked the man what they were for. "'We're just having a meeting here,' the man said. 'If we ever have an epidemic, we need to know what we have on hand.'"

Later that day, Dennis had to go to the base hospital. Noticing a number of ambulances parked outside, he peered in one of them. He saw something like stainless steel. But it had odd-looking pink, purple, and black shadings.

A few minutes later, Dennis stopped in the hospital lounge for a soft drink.

"A captain was there," Dennis says, "leaning against the door. I said, 'Looks like you got a crash.' The captain demanded to know who I was. Then he ordered two MPs to escort me off the base."

The next day Dennis met a friend in a coffee shop. This friend was an army nurse from the hospital. Upset and crying, she told him about the aliens that had been brought to the hospital.

She drew a picture of the aliens on a napkin. They were small creatures, with large heads and eyes. Each hand had four fingers with what looked like suction cups on the tips. A few days later, the nurse was transferred to England.

"I didn't talk about it until 1990," Dennis said. "I just didn't want to get involved. I never told my wife or anybody else. If I'd told this in 1947, who would have believed it, anyway? I didn't want my kids getting made fun of because their old man saw flying things."

Walter Haut was another witness. In 1947, he was an information officer for the army. On July 7, Col. Blanchard told him to write a press release to announce that the army had found a crashed flying saucer.

Haut delivered the press release to two newspapers and two radio stations. Soon the phone was "ringing like mad," he said. Everyone wanted to know more about the flying saucer that had crashed.

A few hours later, he was told to put out a new press release. This one said that the crashed object was actually a weather balloon.

Haut never believed it.

In 1994, the Air Force issued a report about the crash. It said that a weather balloon had indeed crashed near Roswell. But it was a top-secret spy balloon. Its purpose was to search the atmosphere for proof of Soviet nuclear tests.

In 1997, another report came out about the dead bodies of so-called aliens. This report said that the "bodies" were really Air Force test dummies.

But many people aren't convinced. Some, like Loretta Proctor, say, "If we're here, why can't other creatures be out there?"

STRANGE BUT TRUE STORIES

THE DEADLY PORTRAITS

In 1907, Andre Marcellin was a well-known artist in Paris, France. He painted beautiful landscapes—but never portraits. Whenever he was asked, he always refused. "I do not know why," he would say, "but for some reason I have a bad feeling about painting portraits."

One Paris banker, however, was determined to have Marcellin paint his portrait. He wouldn't give in until the reluctant artist finally agreed. Sitting proudly, the banker posed for several days until the portrait was finally finished. Two days later, the banker died.

Marcellin was horrified. For six months, he painted only landscapes. Then, for some unexplained reason, he had the urge to do another portrait. This time, the subject was a young woman.

Again, two days after the portrait was

completed, the young woman died.

Marcellin's friends insisted that the deaths were only a coincidence. To prove it, they encouraged him to paint another portrait. This time, the subject was one of his close friends.

When the picture was finished, Marcellin's friend was delighted. He paid for the portrait and took it home.

Two days later, when nothing had happened, Marcellin was greatly relieved. But on the third day, he heard the tragic news: His friend had died that morning. The man's death had been sudden, and unexpected.

Marcellin decided his portraits were cursed. He vowed never to paint another.

Then, in 1913, Andre Marcellin met a lovely woman. Her name was Francois Noel. Before long Andre and Francois were engaged to be married.

Francois was vain. Wanting a lasting image of her youthful beauty, she begged her fiancé to paint her portrait. Marcellin refused. He didn't dare tempt fate again, so he told her about the curse. But she laughed at him, insisting that his fears were foolish.

Still, he refused to paint her portrait. Finally, she told Marcellin that he *must* paint her portrait—or she wouldn't marry him.

At that point, Andre Marcellin gave in. He painted a beautiful portrait of his fiancée. A week later, the lovely Francois Noel was dead.

For several weeks, Marcellin sat alone, overwhelmed with guilt and despair. He hid in his studio, doing nothing. Then, at last, he began to paint again.

His new work was a self-portrait.

A few days after the painting was finished, Andre Marcellin died.

STRANGE BUT TRUE STORIES

UNDER THE KNIFE— AND LISTENING

Dr. Ronald Katz remembers the terrible aftermath of a certain woman's surgery. During the operation, two doctors were talking. One of them said the woman had the worst case of thyroid cancer he'd ever seen. "She's not going to live very long," he added.

"When the woman woke up from surgery," Katz says, "she repeated, word for word, what the doctors had said." The grim prognosis made her feel suicidal.

"Six months later," Katz went on, "she jumped out of a window and killed herself."

Do people really hear during surgery?

Anesthesia puts many of our senses to sleep. Once we're sedated, we feel no pain, and we cannot remember pain. Our muscles don't move and we can't see. But hearing is the most difficult of all the human senses to block.

Why would that be? For thousands of years, hearing was absolutely necessary to survival. According to Dr. Martin Bogetz, "Even while asleep, humans needed their hearing to stay on the alert from predators."

Dr. Neil Parkinson says, "I'll bet if you asked ten surgeons, nine of them had a patient remember something that was said during surgery."

In 1965, Dr. B.W. Levinson did an experiment. He put 10 patients under deep anesthesia. Then he created a fake crisis. He and another doctor would say things like, "Just a moment! I don't like the patient's color. His/her lips are very blue." None of the 10 patients could remember anything afterward. But under hypnosis, they did. Four patients repeated the exact words. Another four remembered someone talking. And that memory made them anxious.

Psychologist Henry L. Bennett and two colleagues did another experiment. While 11 patients were being operated on, Bennett and his colleagues gave them an order. They told the patients to pull on their ears when they woke up. Most of them did.

Bennett says that some doctors make negative comments about patients during surgery. Perhaps they remark about the patient's looks or say something about the patient being poor or homeless.

Bennett insists that surgeons' careless remarks can kill people. He's seen heart attacks during surgery. He feels the only explanation for those heart attacks is comments made by doctors.

Dr. Katz says doctors "should act as though all patients are awake and can hear. They may not remember every word being said, but the message registers in their brains. And I don't want any remarks like, 'Whoops, I dropped that' or 'Boy, this patient sure is ugly.'"

Sometimes doctors can't avoid talking. Katz puts earphones over his patients' ears so they can listen to music. Some doctors use earplugs.

Other doctors make sure everything they say is positive. During surgery, they tell their patients how well things are going. They assure them they'll recover quickly and without pain.

In one experiment, positive talk seemed to pay off. All the patients in one group listened to music during surgery. The other group was told to relax. Then they were told that how quickly they recovered was up to them. The positive talk seemed to have an effect. The group who heard that message was able to leave the hospital sooner.

Did the other group leave the hospital humming the music they heard? We don't know. It wasn't part of the study.

STRANGE BUT TRUE STORIES

AMAZING ANIMALS

GUINNESS TO THE RESCUE

One day in April 1990, Jess Yates helped a friend build a stone wall. Keeping Jess company was his faithful dog, Guinness. Guinness was a collie/Labrador mix—black, with floppy ears.

That evening, Jess, a diabetic, was really tired. That meant he had to be even more careful than usual about his blood sugar levels.

Jess crawled into bed at 11:00 that night. He was certain that he'd checked his blood sugar, as he always did. And he was very good about keeping emergency foods—such as raisins or soft drinks—at his bedside. If his blood sugar dropped during the night, extra sugar was always close at hand.

But because of exhaustion, Jess just glanced at his bedside table. Seeing his energy drink bottle and some candy bar wrappers, he thought everything was okay.

At 2:30 that morning, Jess woke suddenly. "I was soaking wet. I thought my waterbed had burst," he said. But it wasn't water. Jess was sweating terribly.

He knew he was in trouble. If he didn't raise his blood sugar level soon, he could fall into a coma.

Jess reached for his energy drink, but the bottle was empty. "Never mind," he thought. "I'll have the chocolate." He reached for the candy bars. The wrappers were empty, too!

He knew that several chocolate bars were downstairs on the kitchen counter. Jess tried to get out of bed. But to his horror, he found that he couldn't move his legs! The lack of sugar kept his brain from sending signals to his legs.

"I tried not to panic," Jess said. "The more you panic, the more energy you waste." He grabbed a candy bar wrapper, and called Guinness. His faithful dog hurried over to him. Somehow he seemed to sense that his master was in trouble.

Jess pushed the candy wrapper close to the dog's nose. "Go on, Guinness, fetch!" he said. He prayed that the dog would understand.

To Jess' relief, the big dog ran downstairs. Jess waited, hoping. But Guinness came back with nothing. "That's when I got even more anxious," Jess remembered. "Guinness thought it was all a game."

Jess tried again. He found a bit of chocolate in one of the wrappers and called Guinness once more. This time, he rubbed the chocolate on Guinness's nose.

Guinness knew that he wasn't allowed to take anything without permission. But this time, Jess could only hope that Guinness would make an exception.

Guinness hurried downstairs and was back in seconds. He dropped a familiar black wrapper on the pillow next to Jess.

It was a candy bar! Jess grabbed it and wolfed it down. "It was just enough to get my legs working again," he said. "I managed to get downstairs and have an energy drink."

Soaked in sweat, Jess sat in the dark kitchen. He was shaking—*but he was alive*—because of Guinness. "I picked him up and gave him a big hug," he said. "I probably cried a little, too."

SMOKEY, THE WATCHCAT

Experts have trained many animals to help people with disabilities. But a cat named Smokey taught herself.

Mary and Philip Nabarro lived with their daughter, Jane. All the Nabarros are hearing impaired. They communicate by using sign language and lip-reading.

When Smokey was about 18 months old, the Nabarros noticed something unusual about her. In one way, she acted like a dog! When she wanted something, she'd sit down squarely in front of them.

Animal experts say it's very rare for cats to communicate so directly with their owners.

Smokey seemed to notice that the Nabarros couldn't hear noises in and around their house. So she sat in front of them if the phone or the doorbell rang. She also alerted Jane when she left water running. Once, Smokey warned them of a prowler in their yard. In effect, Smokey became the family's ears.

When Jane went to college in London, she took the cat. "One night," Jane says, "Smokey suddenly came over from the window and looked right up at me. She didn't look very happy, either." It was a small thing, but by now, Jane knew this was a warning. She went up to the window—and saw a strange man peering back at her! For a woman living alone in a big city, this was a frightening moment. "I phoned my boyfriend," Jane says. "He came over and chased the man away."

Once again, a warning from Smokey

had kept a threat to her family from turning into something serious.

Smokey is 13 years old now, and she's still standing guard over her hearing-impaired family.

MERLIN, THE WONDER HORSE

Vicky Jones's riding career almost ended when she was eight years old. That was when she was thrown from a pony and broke her back.

But Vicky was a fighter. Immediately after the accident, she told her father, "I'm not giving up."

The little girl was lucky—as well as determined. After a long, painful year of therapy, she recovered completely. Before long she was physically able to ride again.

The accident, however, had badly shaken Vicky's confidence. "I just froze," she said about the first time she tried to ride again.

Vicky and her mother searched for a new horse. They looked at eight horses, but Vicky didn't like any of them. The ninth horse, though, was different. He was an ugly fellow with a gray coat. His pink nose looked like it had been splashed with paint. His name was Merlin.

Vicky immediately felt comfortable with Merlin. He was the one.

In just a few weeks, the girl who was afraid to get on a horse was jumping fences! The more she and Merlin trained together, the more confident Vicky became. She began to compete—and win.

When Vicky was 12, she made a mistake in a jump—and fell. This was the moment everyone had been dreading. Fortunately, Vicky was unhurt, and the fall didn't bother her at all.

Two weeks later, Vicky's mother noticed something very strange. When Vicky wasn't riding Merlin, he was very clumsy. Sometimes he'd knock down fence poles when jumping. Once he even stepped on Vicky's bike.

A vet gave Merlin several tests. As the testing went on, Merlin's condition became obvious: *He was going blind*.

In fact, Merlin had been nearly blind for at least two years. All this time, he'd been jumping fences and winning prizes. Because he trusted Vicky completely, he'd been guided only by her subtle body movements and soft-spoken commands.

Vicky's mother called a vet who specialized in caring for animals' eyes. Dr. Derek Knottenbelt examined Merlin and found that he had serious cataracts. He also had another very painful eye disease. The vet could operate—but the chance of success was only three percent. If the operation didn't succeed, Merlin would have to be put to sleep.

Vicky was *sure* the operation would succeed. Her mother wasn't sure at all.

When the operation was over, they heard the best possible news: The operation worked! "It's incredible," the vet announced.

Vicky doesn't jump Merlin anymore, but she still rides him and cares for him. She wasn't at all surprised that Merlin had regained most of his vision. "I always knew that Merlin was a very special horse," she said. "And he always will be."

THE LAWN CHAIR PILOT

Was he brave or just boneheaded?

Larry Walters, a 33-year-old truck driver, had dreamed of this stunt for years. On July 2, 1982, he actually did it. After strapping himself in a lawn chair, he zoomed into the sky!

Tied to the lawn chair were 42 six-foot weather balloons filled with helium. Several plastic jugs of water were also attached to the chair. The weight of the water gave the lawn chair ballast. The only other things Walters took along were a parachute, an altimeter, a CB radio, a couple of liters of soda, and a BB pistol.

Walters' strange journey began outside his girlfriend's house in San Pedro, California. First his chair was tied by ropes to the bumper of a friend's car. Then the friend took off at high speed. When the ropes were cut, Walters shot into the sky. As he said later, "I took off so quickly, it knocked my glasses off! I couldn't see very well, but I could tell I was going up fast."

In fact, he was traveling at 1,000 feet per minute! When he reached 16,000 feet, he was high enough. To stop climbing, he took out the BB pistol and shot out some of the balloons.

Pilots of TWA and Delta planes both reported seeing Walters. A control tower chief, Jerry Yocom, said, "We were pretty shocked. We alerted (nearby) aircraft so they'd be able to avoid him."

Walters had hoped to reach the Rocky Mountains. But there was hardly enough wind to take him anywhere. And he was getting very cold. "The cold was the worst thing," he said. "Especially my face and feet. They were freezing."

After almost two hours in the air, Walters was eager to get back to earth. "I started shooting at the balloons with my pellet gun. As each one popped, I'd go a little lower. After a while, I was gliding over the tops of streets and buildings and houses. That was the scariest part. What would I do if I crashed into something? I was especially afraid that my aluminum chair would hit the power lines. Hey—if that happened, I'd get electrocuted!"

In fact, Walters did float *under* some power lines. When the balloons caught on the lines, Walters and his chair swung back and forth. That was enough for him. Carefully easing himself out of his chair, he dropped to the ground—safely.

Later he told a reporter, "It was no death wish—but you couldn't pay me to do it again!"

Soon Walters appeared on the Leno and Letterman shows. He also was fined $1,500 by the Federal Aeronautics Agency for breaking several laws. And he won a "Bonehead of the Year" award from the Bonehead Club in Dallas, Texas.

STRANGE BUT TRUE STORIES

A DREAM COMES TRUE

On May 7, 1915, Marion Holbourne of London, England, fell asleep in an easy chair. She dreamed that she was on a ship that was leaning sharply to one side. It was sinking! Passengers were scrambling to get into lifeboats.

In her dream Mrs. Holbourne wasn't afraid—for herself. But she was *very* frightened for her husband. She couldn't find him anywhere.

She stopped a young officer—a fellow with brown eyes and blond hair. She asked if he'd seen her husband.

"He's fine," the officer said. "I just helped him into a lifeboat."

At this point, Mrs. Holbourne woke up. The dream had scared her badly—for her husband was at sea heading home to England. He was a passenger on the ocean liner *Lusitania*.

Mrs. Holbourne's family told her not to worry about her silly dream.

Then they heard the news: The *Lusitania* had sunk! It had been torpedoed by a German submarine and had gone down in 20 minutes. Of 1,965 passengers aboard, only 764 survived.

One of them was her husband.

When Mr. Holbourne was with his family again, he told them what had happened. "I owe my life to a young officer," he said. "For a while there, I was sure I was going to die. The ship was sinking very fast. But then this officer came to my rescue. He got me to a lifeboat just before the ship went down."

Mrs. Holbourne turned pale. "What did he look like?" she asked. "Do you remember, dear?"

"I'll never forget him," her husband said. "He was a young fellow with blond hair and brown eyes."

Mrs. Holbourne's dream had really come true.

Confederates were furious with Lincoln. He had a great number of enemies. Several times over the years, his life had been threatened.

Lincoln's bodyguard, W.H. Crook, said that the president had three more warning dreams before the night of April 14. Crook also said that Lincoln knew he'd die on the 14th. The bodyguard begged him to stay home from the theater that night. But Lincoln insisted on going. During the play, an actor named John Wilkes Booth sneaked up behind the president and shot him.

For many years, it was rumored that Lincoln's spirit roamed the White House. Several White House staff members reported hearing his footsteps.

Grace Coolidge was the wife of Calvin Coolidge, the thirtieth U.S. president. She said she saw Lincoln's spirit, dressed in black. Across his shoulders he wore a stole, to ward off the chills of the night air.

Theodore Roosevelt, the twenty-sixth

president, said this of Lincoln's spirit: "I see him in the different rooms and halls." Roosevelt's guests sometimes saw him, too. One night, Queen Wilhelmina of the Netherlands stayed in the Rose Room of the White House. She heard a knock on her door. When she opened it, she saw Lincoln's tall figure. He was standing in the hall, wearing a top hat.

Harry S. Truman, the thirty-third president, heard two sharp knocks at his bedroom door early one morning. He opened the door and saw nothing. But he heard footsteps leaving the area. And he said he felt a "cold spot moving away."

The thirty-fourth president, Dwight Eisenhower, was sometimes aware of Lincoln's spirit, too. He told his press secretary, James Haggerty, that he often felt Lincoln's presence.

Lady Bird Johnson was the wife of Lyndon Baines Johnson, the thirty-sixth president. One night, there was a special program on TV about Lincoln's death.

Suddenly, the first lady's press secretary, Liz Carpenter, felt a strange sensation. She felt that someone was compelling her to turn her eyes toward a plaque on the mantel. The writing on the plaque was a quotation from Lincoln! As Liz Carpenter read it, she said she felt "a chill, a draft."

There are also stories about Lincoln's funeral train. When Lincoln was killed, his body was taken to Illinois, the place of his birth, to be buried. All along the railroad tracks, from Washington to Illinois, grieving Americans watched the funeral train pass by.

Some people say the train still rides down the same track. It's draped in black, and driven by skeletons, they say, as it silently passes by.

In life, Lincoln was a troubled man. Even today many believe that his spirit is still not at rest.

FROZEN ALIVE

It was a cold Saturday morning in the month of December 1987. Little Justin Bunker's Connecticut neighborhood was blanketed in snow! To the nine-year-old boy, it looked like a perfect day for a sled ride.

Within an hour Justin and his friend were hauling a sled to a nearby school. A steep hill there was perfect for sledding.

They took a shortcut by going through an opening in a chain-link fence around an outdoor swimming pool. As they walked around the pool, they noticed that it was covered with ice.

The ice looked solid. The boys began to "skate" on the ice in their heavy boots. Then they began to jump around.

Suddenly, the ice cracked under Justin's feet. With a yell, he slipped under the icy water. His horrified friend crept up to the hole and stared into the dark water. It looked like Justin was lying on the bottom of the pool. He was face up, and he wasn't moving!

The boy raced to tell Justin's mother, who called the fire department. In six minutes, firefighters and paramedics arrived at the pool. Two rescue workers jumped in. The water was dark and their clothes were heavy. Since it was so hard to see, several minutes passed before they reached Justin.

It took many more minutes to pull Justin out of the pool. His body was stiff. His eyes were frozen shut. His lungs and stomach were partly filled with icy water. By now, he'd been underwater for more than 20 minutes. It seemed that Justin Bunker was dead.

Yet Justin still had a pulse—a faint one. He was rushed to the hospital. There, they put an oxygen mask over his face and wrapped his whole body in an electric heating pad. For eight hours, he lay there, without moving at all.

Then, astounding everyone, Justin sat up in bed! Nurses rushed to his side as the boy pulled off the oxygen mask. "Hey, what's going on?" he cried out. "What happened?"

A few weeks later, Justin was well enough to go home. Against all odds, he'd recovered completely.

Was it a miracle? How did Justin survive being trapped underwater for more than 20 minutes?

A person plunged in icy water can be "quick frozen." Blood vessels near the skin shut down. The brain and other organs cool down quickly. The heart beats so slowly, it seems to stop. When Justin Bunker fell into the pool, he was "quick frozen."

Strange as it seems, quite a few people have survived an experience like Justin's.

STRANGE BUT TRUE STORIES

PUZZLING PLACES

THE MEGALITHS

Megaliths are prehistoric monuments found in many parts of the world. They're made of giant stones, carefully arranged in patterns. Individually, some of these stones weigh several tons.

Who built the megaliths? How did they do it? And especially—*why* did these ancient people build them?

Most megaliths are in Britain, Ireland, Spain, France, Portugal, Scandinavia, and Algeria. In fact, there are about 50,000 megaliths in these areas. At Carnac, France, one megalith is made from 10,000 stones. The Carnac stones stand in straight rows, like a marching army.

Perhaps the most famous megalith is Stonehenge, in England. This structure consists of two great circles, one inside the other. The circles are made of *enormous* upright stones. Some of them weigh as much as 50 tons! We now know that the stones came from 20 miles away.

How did human beings ever move such huge stones? Some think that megaliths such as Stonehenge were built by beings from other planets. They believe that megaliths are guides to help spacecraft land safely on Earth.

But science tells us that Stonehenge was built by early humans, between 3100 and 1100 B.C. At that time, the wheel had not yet been invented. We have trouble imagining how early people carried these stones over such a distance. However they did it, it was an amazing feat!

And we still don't know *why* the megaliths were built. Some of them seem to have been temples. Others were tombs. Many megaliths show signs that people and animals were once sacrificed there.

Even today, visitors claim to feel energy from a megalith. They say the earth itself seems alive at that spot.

Experts have studied the megaliths for many years. In 1966, an astronomer named Gerald Hawkins measured the distances between the stones. Then he fed the results into a computer. From that information he decided there was a connection between the position of the stones and the movements of the planets. Perhaps the structures told farmers the best time to plant crops.

A Scottish engineer, Alexander Thom, developed a similar theory. He found connections between several megaliths and the movements of the sun, moon, and stars.

Many studies suggest that megaliths *do* have a certain type of energy. Researchers found that many megaliths were built over deposits of uranium. Were the megalith-builders attracted to spots that were naturally radioactive?

For centuries, people believed the megaliths had the power to heal. In Cornwall, England, for example, there's a megalith shaped like a huge doughnut. Sick children were passed through the hole of the stone "doughnut" to be cured!

Some researchers have found that certain stones have very high levels of magnetic energy. Do the stones truly have the power to heal? In some hospitals today, electromagnetism is used to help broken bones mend.

Will the mystery of the megaliths ever be solved? If so, the stones may reveal more about people from the past. Perhaps they will also carry a message for men and women in today's world.

THE BERMUDA TRIANGLE

A number of ships and planes have disappeared in the Bermuda Triangle. This area of ocean is bounded by Miami, Florida; San Juan, Puerto Rico; and the island of Bermuda. The mystery is that most of these ships and planes vanished without a trace! And in most cases, there was no call for help. Searchers have never been able to find any survivors or wreckage of the missing planes or ships.

Perhaps the most famous case was one called the "Lost Patrol."

It was December 5, 1945, just a few months after World War II had ended. Five torpedo bombers carrying 14 men left Fort Lauderdale Naval Air Station. The men were on a practice bombing run. Their leader was Lt. Charles Taylor, 28. He was a combat veteran with 2,500 hours of flying time.

The squadron took off at 2:10 P.M. At 3:40 P.M., Taylor radioed the naval air station, saying that he was in trouble. He wasn't sure where he was.

Two hours later, an air station in Miami helped to locate the squadron. Taylor turned the planes toward shore.

In the meantime, however, a storm had blown up. And worse yet, the five bombers were almost out of fuel.

At 5:22 P.M., Taylor radioed the other planes: "When the first plane gets down to 10 gallons of gas, we'll all land our planes in the water together. Does everyone understand that?"

The last radio call from Taylor was at 7:04. But the transmission was too weak to be understood.

At 7:27 P.M., a seaplane was sent to look for any survivors among the 14 men. Then at 7:50, a ship reported seeing the plane explode.

The next four days saw one of the biggest air searches in history. Some 200 planes, from 11 different naval air stations, were sent to join the search. Their surveillance covered a 200,000-square-mile area. No one found a trace of the squadron.

More than a few people think the squadron was abducted by aliens. But there are more logical explanations. The Gulf Stream in the triangle area is extremely fast moving. Wreckage from planes and ships could easily be swept away. Also, the ocean floor in that area features some of the deepest trenches in the world. Buried deep in a trench, a wrecked plane or ship would be very difficult to find.

And storms can develop very quickly in the triangle area. A ship or plane may not have a chance to call for help.

The Bermuda Triangle is also called the "Devil's Triangle." A similar place exists off the east coast of Japan. Many sea and air crafts have disappeared there, too. That place is called the "Devil's Sea."

ENORMOUS IMAGES ON THE EARTH

WYOMING'S GIANT WHEEL

High in the mountains of Wyoming lies a "wheel" made of stones. Stones form its rim, hub, and spokes. At each end of the wheel, there are piles of rocks. The wheel is enormous—82 feet in diameter.

There are other such curious wheels in Canada and Arizona. And there are dozens more across the great plains of the United States. Some are only a few feet across. Others are hundreds of times larger. Like the Wyoming wheel, they are all positioned on high ground. The Wyoming wheel, however, is the best preserved.

Who built these puzzling structures— and *why*?

Scientists think the Wyoming wheel was made in the 1100s. The builders, they believe, were the Native Americans of the plains. But why were they built? The rock piles at the Wyoming wheel give us some clues. They mark the summer solstice. The sun rises over one of the rock piles on the morning of the solstice. A second pile marks the sunset of that day. Other piles mark the appearance of certain stars as the season changes. Since the wheels were all built on high ground, they offer a clear view of the horizon.

Some believe these stone images are a lot like the megaliths in other parts of the world.

But the mystery remains. The Native Americans of the plains did not plant crops. They hunted buffalo and followed the great herds of the plains. So why would they need to know when the seasons changed? Perhaps the solstice marked a time when the buffalo were on the move.

But no one knows for sure. Perhaps we may never know.

OHIO'S GREAT SERPENT MOUND

It was 1975. The Ohio Valley was warm that sunny November afternoon. But Robert W. Harner was filled with cold dread. "I felt the hair rising on the nape of my neck," he said. "I could neither move nor speak. Although I was by myself, I knew I was not *really* alone."

Harner was standing on a high mound of earth known as the Great Serpent. Although there was no wind, he watched, terrified, as the leaves below him began to move. One by one, and then in groups, the leaves climbed toward him in an unnatural way. In fact, *they rose as if they were walking*. When they were 15 or 20 feet away, the leaves formed one group and whirled around and around Harner.

Finally, Harner turned toward his car to get his camera. But at that moment, the spell was broken. "I saw that the leaves were already walking back down the hillside," he said. "I knew I could never get back in time to photograph them.

I felt that I'd touched a part of a world I didn't believe existed."

Harner was standing on a sacred spot. The Great Serpent Mound was built some time between 1000 B.C. and A.D. 200 by early Native Americans, called the Adena. Other early Native Americans, such as the Hopewell and the Mississippians, also built mounds. Throughout the United States and Canada, thousands of mounds were built in the shapes of panthers, birds, bears, and other animals.

The mounds are burial places. Many hold gifts to the dead such as beads, weapons, pots, and pipes. The mounds were built before Native Americans used horses or oxen. So the earth used to make them—sometimes several tons of it—was carried on their backs.

Why did the Native Americans pick these particular spots? Robert Harner has his own theory: "Somehow they must have known that very special things happen there."

STRANGE
BUT TRUE STORIES

AMERICA'S PSYCHIC

Jeane Dixon was America's most famous psychic. At the height of her fame, she received thousands of letters every day. More than 800 newspapers carried her horoscope column. Her predictions were read by millions.

Her most famous prediction was made in 1952. As Jeane Dixon tells it, she had a vision—a picture formed in her mind. She saw a handsome young man with blue eyes and thick brown hair who lived in the White House. He was a Democrat, elected in 1960. And he would die while in office.

In 1956, *Parade* magazine printed her prediction. Four years later, in 1960, blue-eyed, brown-haired Democrat John F. Kennedy was elected president. He was the youngest man ever elected.

On Nov. 22, 1963, Dixon was having

lunch at the Mayflower Hotel in Washington, D.C. Two witnesses heard her say, "Something dreadful is going to happen to the president today."

In hours the announcement came: President Kennedy had been shot. Dixon was terribly upset. Her friends tried to assure her that the president would probably be all right.

But Dixon said, "No. We will soon learn that the president is dead."

Dixon was already well-known. But with the prediction of Kennedy's death, her fame soared. She was invited to parties all over Washington, D.C. At every party, people would give Dixon their business cards, asking her to pray for them. Sometimes she made predictions by touching people's fingertips. Often she appeared on television, which was just becoming popular. Soon she became the subject of two best-selling books. When Jeane Dixon had something to say, plenty of people listened.

Born in 1918, Jeane Dixon was the child of wealthy German immigrants. As the story goes, her mother took her eight-year-old daughter to a fortune teller. Saying that the girl had a gift for seeing the future, the fortune teller gave her a crystal ball. Dixon kept the fortune teller's gift for many years.

Another childhood story concerns her grandfather. One day she asked her mother about a letter edged in black. Her mother was puzzled; there was no such letter. Yet a few days later, a black-edged letter—containing the sad news of her grandfather's death—arrived in the mail.

During World War II, Dixon offered astrological predictions to servicemen. The men felt that her predictions were accurate. Soon Dixon was getting mail from many others, asking her to foretell their future.

In 1944, President Franklin D. Roosevelt invited her to the White House. Dixon said the president asked her how long he had to finish his work. Dixon's reply was, "Less than six months." In fact, he died just three months later.

Many more of her predictions proved to be accurate. As early as 1952, she predicted the race riots of the early 1960s. In 1960, she predicted Martin Luther King would be murdered. She also predicted that both Richard Nixon and Ronald Reagan would be elected president of the United States.

Jeane Dixon amazed people by foretelling the 1964 earthquake in Alaska, and the fall of the Berlin Wall. And nine months before it happened, she said that actress Marilyn Monroe would kill herself.

Many predictions, though, did *not* come true. Dixon prophesied that a woman would be elected president in the 1980s, and that World War III would begin in 1958. She predicted the Soviet Union would be first to put a man on the moon. And she also said that President

George H.W. Bush would be elected to a second term. (But Bush lost to Clinton.)

Dixon explained her failures by saying that she hadn't read the signs correctly. Besides astrology, she used dreams, mind reading, and "inner voices" to make her predictions. She once described what it was like to have a vision. She said it felt as if she were "surrounded by whipped cream . . . I sense peacefulness and love . . . I feel like I'm looking down from a higher planet . . . and I'm wondering why others can't see what I'm seeing."

Eventually, Jeane Dixon's popularity faded. Many newspapers stopped running her horoscope column. But even as late as the 1990s, First Lady Nancy Reagan was asking her advice.

Many called Dixon a crackpot. Some said her only talent was to make herself rich and famous. But many who knew her thought otherwise.

For one thing, Dixon never took

money for her predictions. (She felt she would lose her gift if she profited from it.) She took in stray dogs and cats, and her vet bills were huge. She cooked meals for blind and elderly people and invited many runaway children and pregnant teenagers to stay with her.

Dixon died of a heart attack at age 79. If she had predicted her death, she never said so out loud.

When Dixon's fame was greatest, astrology was very popular. It is far less popular now. Many people insist they don't believe in astrology. But some of these same people just might be reading their daily horoscope—when no one's looking.

STRANGE BUT TRUE STORIES

MYSTERIES IN THE SKY

It happened just after midnight on September 19, 1976. Witnesses calling the military center in Tehran, Iran, reported seeing an enormous ball of light. They said its brilliant colors changed from white to orange to violet. The unidentified flying object (UFO) was hovering on the outskirts of Tehran.

An officer from the center called Shahrokhi Air Base. Lieutenant Jafari, 23, was ordered to go after the UFO. At 1:30 A.M., Jafari took off in an F4 Phantom fighter plane. When he was just a few miles away, the UFO suddenly shot away. Jafari couldn't keep up with it. When he called the base, they told him to turn around and come back.

Then, a few moments later, the base heard the terrified pilot say, "Something is coming at me from behind! It's 15 miles away . . . now 10 miles . . . now it's 5 . . . I think it's going to crash into me . . ."

The listeners at the base waited anxiously. Then they heard Jafari saying, "It's passed me by—narrowly missing me!"

The experience left Jafari shaken and confused. Another pilot had to guide him back to the base. Later, Jafari said that his communications instruments lost power when he tried to close in on the UFO. But when he stopped the chase, his instruments began working again.

Had Jafari received a *warning*?

By now, the base had sent off a second Phantom. Traveling several hundred miles per hour, it would reach the UFO in about 9 minutes. The pilot had locked on his radar intercept equipment. There was no way he could miss the glowing ball.

It was then that the UFO seemed to go into high gear. The Phantom was going all out, but it couldn't come close to the UFO's amazing speed!

Then, without warning, the UFO shot

out a bolt of light, turned, and headed straight for the Phantom!

Instantly, the pilot threw a switch to fire off an AIM9 missile. *But nothing happened.* The missile wouldn't launch. In fact, the entire weapons system was dead.

Meanwhile, the bolt from the UFO was still headed for the Phantom. To avoid it, the pilot dove sharply. But the bolt dove, too—still heading for the defenseless plane. The pilot and navigator prepared to eject.

Then, just before impact, the bolt made an amazing u-turn. Suddenly it was headed straight for the UFO again.

A few seconds later, the plane's weapons system came back to life. But the shaken pilot didn't even try to launch another missile.

As the Phantom pulled out of its dive, the UFO shot off a second bolt of light. This time, however, the bolt streaked straight down to earth.

The Phantom crew braced for an

explosion. But it never came. Instead, the light settled on the desert floor. There, it simply glowed, lighting up the land as if it were midday.

The Phantom's two-man crew was ordered to take a closer look. So the pilot dropped from 25,000 feet to 15,000. He and the navigator could see nothing solid inside the brilliant glow. But from time to time, the Phantom's communication system went dead. A commercial airplane nearby was reporting the same problem.

Suddenly, the brilliant light died out, and the sky went completely black. Now the pilot could hardly see. The intense light had nearly blinded him. He had to circle the night sky for an hour before he could land safely.

The U.S. Secretary of Defense wrote a report of the incident. He said the encounter was highly believable. He also suggested that such UFO incidents should be studied further. But his report was kept secret until many years later.

• • •

Since the 1950s, the U.S. government has been keeping secret reports of UFO incidents. Only recently, because of the Freedom of Information Act, has the public been able to read these reports.

UFOs have been reported since World War II. During the war, pilots reported strange lights traveling at the same speed as their planes. There have been reports of UFOs all over the world.

Most UFOs have similar qualities. They are silent, wingless, and faster than any plane on earth. Our most agile plane can't bounce, zoom, zigzag, or dive like UFOs. Reports say these spacecraft are lit with bright oranges, greens, whites, and multicolored flashes. Unlike UFOs in movies, they don't shoot back.

Opinion polls show that almost half of Americans believe that UFOs are from outer space. Scientists, though, demand more solid evidence. And they want to learn more about space. They already know that space is alive with different types of energy. These energies could produce objects that we can't see. Yet sometimes people *do* see them.

In November 1986, Kenju Terauchi was flying a cargo plane. As he flew near Fairbanks, Alaska, he saw two strange objects. They were the size of smaller airplanes, he said, but they didn't look or move like any airplane.

Then he saw the outline of a huge, ringed object. To Terauchi, it looked as large as two aircraft carriers!

The radar from Terauchi's plane picked up the object. Radar on the ground also tracked the strange object as it kept pace with Terauchi's plane. When he circled, the object stayed with him.

Then another airliner appeared. As Terauchi signaled it, the object went dark.

John Callahan was then an accident investigator for the Federal Aviation Administration. He studied the radar records. To Callahan, they indicated that a UFO had indeed been in the sky. But he never had a chance to complete his investigation. The records were taken away by the Central Intelligence Agency. Callahan says the CIA agent told him and other FAA investigators, "All of you are sworn to secrecy. Do you understand? *This event never happened*."

Callahan asked the CIA agent what *he* thought the pilot saw.

According to Callahan, the agent replied, "It's a UFO. But we can't tell the American public we're being visited by UFOs. It would scare the life out of 'em."

STRANGE BUT TRUE STORIES

STEER CLEAR OF THESE ADDRESSES!

OPRAH WINFREY'S HARPO STUDIOS

The building at 110 N. Carpenter St. in Chicago is now the home of Oprah Winfrey's Harpo Studios. But that street address has a sad history. At one time the building was the Second Regiment Armory. In July 1915, hundreds of dead and dying people were brought there after the *Eastland* tragedy.

The *S.S. Eastland* was an excursion ship. On July 24, 1915, she was loaded with more than 2,500 passengers bound for their company picnic. The *Eastland* was scheduled to take them across Lake Michigan to Michigan City.

The *Eastland* never left the wharf. Instead, it rolled over, dumping terrified men, women, and children into the water. More than 800 people died.

The bodies were taken to the Second Regiment Armory. They were laid out in long rows, so family members could identify them. After seven days, all the bodies had been identified.

In 1998, Oprah Winfrey bought the building. She'd heard stories that the place was haunted. But that didn't stop her from turning it into a studio for *The Oprah Winfrey Show*.

When asked about the place being haunted, Winfrey refuses to answer. But there have been stories. Some employees say they've been mysteriously locked in their own offices. Others talk about light switches being turned back on when no one is around. And some employees even report seeing spirits.

Once, a security guard was walking through the halls. Suddenly, he smelled perfume. He looked around, but didn't see anyone. When he returned to the security center, other guards asked him why he hadn't stopped the unauthorized female visitor. They'd all seen her—and so had several security cameras!

For years, Oprah Winfrey wouldn't talk about Harpo Studios being haunted. But in 1996, during a taping of *Oprah*, she finally did. "There have been sightings of extraterrestrial people," she admitted. "That's why you won't ever find me here after midnight."

THE GHOSTS OF DRURY LANE

Drury Lane is a very old theater in London. Over the years, dozens of people claim to have seen ghosts there. The most famous is called "the Man in Gray."

Some believe the Man in Gray is the spirit of a dead man found in the theater. Over a century ago, building workers broke though a wall in the upper balcony. There they found a skeleton—with a dagger through its ribs. Bits of cloth were still clinging to the skeleton. When the material was analyzed, the results verified that the dead person had lived and died in the eighteenth century.

Several people have described the Man in Gray. They say that along with his old-fashioned clothes, he wears a powdered wig. And he carries a sword under his long, gray cloak.

The Man in Gray keeps a strict schedule. He's seen only between the hours of 9:00 A.M. and 6:00 P.M. Usually, he shows up during rehearsals and matinees. Then he appears on one end of the balcony and disappears into the wall on the other side. If anyone comes too close to him, he fades away instantly.

Is the Man in Gray the fellow who was murdered? He doesn't seem to be seeking revenge. In fact, theater people feel he is good luck. He often appears at plays that become big hits.

The theater has other ghosts, as well. King Charles II was seen at Drury Lane in 1948. (He'd always loved the theater.)

The theater also has invisible ghosts. A young actress named Betty Jo Jones, an

American, had a comic part in *Oklahoma*. But the audience didn't think she was very funny. During one performance, she felt someone gently guiding her into another position. Who was it? She looked, but no one was around her. As the show went on, she continued to feel gentle hands guiding her around the stage. Her performance improved! The next night, thanks to the guide, her performance improved even more. She felt the guide give her a pat on the back!

The same thing happened to an actress named Doreen Duke. She was terribly nervous about trying out for a part in *The King and I.* But when she got on stage, she, too, felt hands guiding her. And she, too, felt someone give her a pat on the back. She got the part.

In the 1950s, someone offered to exorcise Drury Lane of its ghosts. As you might guess, the offer was refused without a second thought!

STRANGE BUT TRUE STORIES

WHAT A WAY TO GO!

WATCH OUT FOR FLYING MANHOLE COVERS!

In 1989, a great amount of gas became trapped inside a sewer in New York. When the gas exploded, a manhole cover was hurtled 30 feet into the air. Two people were killed.

In 1990, an entire train in Detroit was knocked off its rails. The cause was an underground explosion. The force of the eruption caused several manhole covers to shoot up from the road. That's what derailed the train.

AN UNWELCOME RIDE

In 1994, at a scenic spot in Colorado, a man used his cell phone to call his wife. But, for some reason, the signal from the phone made a nearby wheelchair start up. The wheelchair went over a cliff, along with its frightened passenger!

A DEADLY UMBRELLA

If he'd known what was coming, Georgi Markov would have taken a taxi.

On September 3, 1978, he was patiently waiting at a bus stop. Then, suddenly, a stranger jabbed him in the leg with an umbrella.

Markov was a Bulgarian who lived in England. He didn't like the Bulgarian government. In fact, he spoke out on radio shows every week, criticizing the government. As a result, Markov had made some powerful enemies.

After being jabbed by the umbrella, Markov became terribly ill. Four days later, he was dead—of blood poisoning. The doctors told investigators from Scotland Yard that they found a BB stuck in Markov's leg. That umbrella had been rigged as a pellet gun! The pellet that punctured Markov's leg had been packed with ricin, a deadly poison. One tiny dose had been enough to kill Georgi Markov.

Ricin is made from the castor bean.

Of all the natural poisons, it is the most deadly. Ricin has been used since ancient times. During World War I, it was a major weapon used in chemical warfare.

Later, it was found that Markov had been murdered by a member of the Bulgarian Secret Service. The agent had been clever indeed. What could look more harmless than an umbrella?

DEATH BY MOLASSES

People in Boston's north end had worried about the tank ever since it was built. It contained millions of gallons of molasses—and it leaked constantly. The tank was huge: 58 feet high and 240 feet around. The north end of Boston was an area full of warehouses and wharves. The tank was located close to the harbor, so the molasses could be loaded onto ships.

Owned by Purity Distilling Co., the tank had been built in a hurry. The man in charge had been promised a promotion if he could build it fast. World War I was at its height, and molasses was in demand. This molasses wouldn't be used in gingerbread. Instead, it would be distilled into industrial alcohol for use in weapons factories.

The tank was painted brown so the leaks wouldn't show as much.

Besides industrial alcohol, molasses was used to make rum. As 1919 began, Prohibition was about to become law. Purity Distilling Co. was in a rush to make one last batch of alcohol before it was banned. So they overfilled the tank with 2.5 million gallons of molasses.

The next day, a low rumble shook houses and wharves near the tank. Then people heard loud popping noises like machine gun fire as the tank split apart.

Huge pieces of cast iron knocked a firehouse to the ground. A one-ton piece of steel hit an elevated train trestle, ripping it in half.

Then a wave of steaming-hot molasses, 15 feet high, roared from the tank. Buildings were crushed and freight cars were tossed aside like matches. The sticky liquid filled basements and poured into Boston Harbor, turning the water brown.

Finally, the roaring river of molasses became a slow stream. On Commercial Street the brown goop was three feet deep.

Rescuers went to work. In all, 21 people died that day, as well as 12 horses. More than 150 people were injured. Millions of dollars were lost in damaged buildings and businesses.

For a long time, the brown goop seeped out of cracks in the sidewalk and streets. And for almost 30 years, especially on hot days, the people of north Boston could smell the thick, sweet stink of molasses.